CW00386083

Wisdom
for the
Ages

Wisdom for the Ages

Compiled by
Olivia Warburton

LION
Publishing

This edition copyright © 2000 Lion Publishing

Published by
Lion Publishing plc
Sandy Lane West, Oxford, England
www.lion-publishing.co.uk
ISBN 0 7459 4417 5

First edition 2000
10 9 8 7 6 5 4 3 2 1 0

Published in association with
National Gallery Publications,
5/6 Pall Mall East, London SW1Y 5BA

All illustrations reproduced courtesy of the
Trustees of the National Gallery, London

All rights reserved

A catalogue record for this book is available
from the British Library

Typeset in 11/14 Caslon OldFace
Printed and bound in Singapore

Because I live, you also will live.

Jesus Christ

Introduction

'I am the light of the world,' Jesus said. 'Whoever follows me will never walk in darkness, but will have the light of life.'

Throughout the centuries, the life and teaching of Jesus Christ have influenced different cultures across the world, bringing joy and peace to countless people.

This book tells the story of his life through quotations from the gospel accounts and devotional poetry, beautifully illustrated with details from paintings in the National Gallery collection.

The message of Jesus can still challenge and inspire us today, and his words offer wisdom and hope for the future.

The Annunciation

My soul doth magnify the Lord:
and my spirit hath rejoiced
in God my Saviour:
For he that is mighty
hath magnified me:
and holy is his Name.

The Book of Common Prayer

God sent the angel Gabriel to a town in Galilee
named Nazareth. He had a message for a young
woman promised in marriage to a man named
Joseph, who was a descendent of King David.
Her name was Mary. The angel said to her,
'Don't be afraid, Mary; God has been gracious
to you. You will become pregnant and give birth
to a son, and you will name him Jesus. He will
be great and will be called the Son of the Most
High God.'

Gaudenzio Ferrari,
The Annunciation: The Angel Gabriel

The Nativity

Awake, glad heart! get up and sing!
It is the birthday of thy King.
'Christ's Nativity', Henry Vaughan

At that time the Emperor Augustus ordered a census to be taken throughout the Roman Empire. Everyone, then, went to register himself, each to his own town. Joseph went from the town of Nazareth in Galilee to the town of Bethlehem in Judea, the birthplace of King David. He went to register with Mary, who was promised in marriage to him. She was pregnant, and while they were in Bethlehem, the time came for her to have her baby. She gave birth to her first son, wrapped him in strips of cloth and laid him in a manger – there was no room for them to stay in the inn.

Sandro Botticelli,
'Mystic Nativity'

The Presentation of Jesus

The childhood shows the man,
As morning shows the day.
'Paradise Regained', John Milton

At that time there was a man named Simeon living in Jerusalem. The Holy Spirit had assured him that he would not die before he had seen the Lord's promised Messiah. Led by the Spirit, Simeon went into the Temple. When the parents brought the child Jesus into the Temple to do for him what the Law required, Simeon took the child in his arms and gave thanks to God: 'Now, Lord, you have kept your promise, and you may let your servant go in peace. With my own eyes I have seen your salvation.'

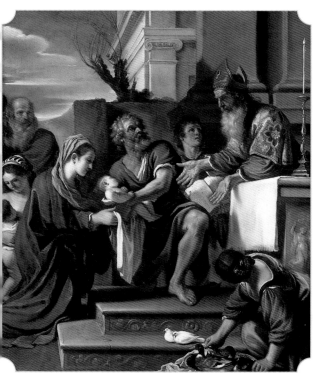

Guercino,
The Presentation of Jesus in the Temple

Jesus Among the Teachers

He in his age's morning thus began
By miracles exceeding power of man.
'La Corona', John Donne

Every year the parents of Jesus went to Jerusalem
for the Passover Festival. When Jesus was twelve
years old, they went to the festival as usual. When
the festival was over, they started back home, but
the boy Jesus stayed in Jerusalem. His parents
did not know this; they thought that he was with
the group, so they travelled a whole day and then
started looking for him among their relatives and
friends. They did not find him, so they went back
to Jerusalem looking for him. On the third day
they found him in the Temple, sitting with the
Jewish teachers, listening to them and asking
questions. All who heard him were amazed at his
intelligent answers.

Lodovico Mazzolino,
Christ disputing with the Doctors

The Baptism of Jesus

What if earth
Be but the shadow of heaven, and things therein
Each to other like, more than on earth is thought?
'Paradise Lost', John Milton

John the Baptist came to the desert of Judea and started preaching. 'Turn away from your sins,' he said, 'because the Kingdom of heaven is near!' Jesus arrived from Galilee and came to John at the Jordan to be baptized by him. But John tried to make him change his mind. 'I ought to be baptized by you,' John said, 'and yet you have come to me!' But Jesus answered him, 'Let it be so for now. For in this way we shall do all that God requires.' So John agreed. As soon as Jesus was baptized, he came up out of the water. Then heaven was opened to him, and he saw the Spirit of God coming down like a dove and alighting on him.

Piero della Francesca,
The Baptism of Christ

The Wedding at Cana

Love is that liquor sweet and most divine,
Which my God feels as blood; but I, as wine.
'The Agonie', George Herbert

There was a wedding in the town of Cana in
Galilee. Jesus' mother was there, and Jesus and
his disciples had also been invited to the wedding.
When the wine had given out, Jesus' mother said
to him, 'They have no wine left.' Jesus said to the
servants, 'Fill these jars with water.' They filled
them to the brim, and then he told them, 'Now
draw some water out and take it to the man in
charge of the feast.' They took him the water,
which now had turned into wine, and he tasted
it. He called the bridegroom and said to him,
'Everyone else serves the best wine first. But you
have kept the best wine until now!'

Mattia Preti,
The Marriage at Cana

The Transfiguration

I saw Eternity the other night
Like a great ring of pure and endless light,
All calm, as it was bright.
'The World', Henry Vaughan

Jesus took Peter, John, and James with him and went up a hill to pray. While he was praying, his face changed its appearance, and his clothes became dazzling white. Suddenly two men were there talking with him. They were Moses and Elijah, who appeared in heavenly glory and talked with Jesus about the way in which he would soon fulfil God's purpose by dying in Jerusalem. A cloud appeared and covered them with its shadow; and the disciples were afraid as the cloud came over them. A voice said from the cloud, 'This is my Son, whom I have chosen – listen to him!'

Duccio,
The Transfiguration

Mary and Martha

And know you not, says Love, who bore the blame?
My dear, then I will serve.
You must sit down, says Love, and taste my meat:
So I did sit and eat.

'Love', George Herbert

As Jesus and his disciples went on their way, he came to a village where a woman named Martha welcomed him in her home. She had a sister named Mary, who sat down at the feet of the Lord and listened to his teaching. Martha was upset over all the work she had to do, so she came and said, 'Lord, don't you care that my sister has left me to do all the work by myself? Tell her to come and help me!' The Lord answered her, 'Martha, Martha! You are worried and troubled over so many things, but just one is needed. Mary has chosen the right thing, and it will not be taken away from her.'

Diego Velázquez,
Kitchen Scene with Christ
in the House of Martha and Mary

The Adulterous Woman

Wilt thou forgive those sins through which I run,
And do them still, though still I do deplore?
'A Hymn to God the Father', John Donne

Jesus went back to the Temple. The teachers of
the Law and the Pharisees brought in a woman
who had been caught committing adultery, and
they made her stand before them all. 'Teacher,'
they said to Jesus, 'this woman was caught in
the very act of committing adultery. In our Law
Moses commanded that such a woman must be
stoned to death. Now, what do you say?' He said
to them, 'Whichever one of you has committed
no sin may throw the first stone at her.' When
they heard this, they all left, one by one.

Rembrandt,
The Woman taken in Adultery

The Raising of Lazarus

One short sleep past, we wake eternally,
And death shall be no more,
Death thou shalt die.

'Death be not proud', John Donne

A man named Lazarus, who lived in Bethany, was ill. Bethany was the town where Mary and her sister Martha lived. The sisters sent Jesus a message: 'Lord, your dear friend is ill.' When Jesus arrived, he found that Lazarus had been buried four days before. As soon as Mary saw him, she fell at his feet. 'Lord,' she said, 'if you had been here, my brother would not have died!' Jesus went to the tomb, which was a cave with a stone placed at the entrance. 'Take the stone away!' Jesus ordered. He called out in a loud voice, 'Lazarus, come out!' He came out, his hands and feet wrapped in grave clothes, and with a cloth round his face. 'Untie him,' Jesus told them, 'and let him go.'

Sebastiano del Piombo,
The Raising of Lazarus

The Entry into Jerusalem

Prayer the Church's banquet, angel's age,
God's breath in man returning to his birth.

'Prayer', George Herbert

When Jesus entered Jerusalem, the whole city
was thrown into an uproar. 'Who is he?' the people
asked. 'This is the prophet Jesus, from Nazareth
in Galilee,' the crowds answered. Jesus went into
the Temple and drove out all those who were buying

and selling there. He overturned the tables of the moneychangers and the stools of those who sold pigeons, and said to them, 'It is written in the Scriptures that God said, "My Temple will be called a house of prayer." But you are making it a hideout for thieves!' The blind and the crippled came to him in the Temple, and he healed them.

After Michelangelo, The Purification of the Temple

The Last Supper

Teach me how to repent; for that's as good
As if thou hadst sealed my pardon, with thy blood.

'At the round earth's imagined corners', John Donne

When it was evening, Jesus came with the twelve disciples. While they were at the table eating, Jesus said, 'I tell you that one of you will betray me – one who is eating with me.' While they were eating, Jesus took a piece of bread, gave a prayer of thanks, broke it, and gave it to his disciples. 'Take it,' he said, 'this is my body.' Then he took a cup, gave thanks to God, and handed it to them; and they all drank from it. Jesus said, 'This is my blood which is poured out for many, my blood which seals God's covenant. I tell you, I will never again drink this wine until the day I drink the new wine in the Kingdom of God.' Then they sang a hymn and went out to the Mount of Olives.

Ercole de' Roberti,
The Institution of the Eucharist

The Agony in the Garden

Arise, arise, they come. Look how they run.
Alas! what haste they make to be undone!
'The Sacrifice', George Herbert

They came to a place called Gethsemane, and
Jesus said to his disciples, 'Sit here while I pray.'
He went a little farther on, threw himself on the
ground, and prayed that, if possible, he might
not have to go through that time of suffering.
'Father,' he prayed, 'my Father! All things are
possible for you. Take this cup of suffering away
from me. Yet not what I want, but what you want.'
Then he came back to the disciples and found
them asleep. He said to them, 'Enough! The hour
has come! Look, here is the man who is betraying
me!' Jesus was still speaking when Judas arrived.
With him was a crowd armed with swords and
clubs, and sent by the chief priests, the teachers
of the Law, and the elders.

Andrea Mantegna,
The Agony in the Garden

The Trial Before Caiaphas

Some said, that I the Temple to the floor
In three days razed, and raised as before.
Why, he that built the world can do much more.
'The Sacrifice', George Herbert

Then Jesus was taken to the High Priest's house.
The High Priest questioned Jesus, 'Have you no
answer to the accusation they bring against you?'
But Jesus kept quiet and would not say a word.
Again the High Priest questioned him, 'Are you
the Messiah, the Son of the Blessed God?' 'I am,'
answered Jesus, 'and you will all see the Son of
Man seated on the right of the Almighty and
coming with the clouds of heaven!' The High
Priest tore his robes and said, 'We don't need any
more witnesses! You heard his blasphemy. What
is your decision?' They all voted against him: he
was guilty and should be put to death.

Gerrit van Honthorst,
Christ before the High Priest

The Trial Before Pilate

Hark how they cry aloud still, Crucify:
It is not fit he live a day, they cry,
Who cannot live less than eternally.
'The Sacrifice', George Herbert

The whole group rose up and took Jesus before
Pilate, where they began to accuse him: 'We
caught this man misleading our people, telling
them not to pay taxes to the Emperor and
claiming that he himself is the Messiah, a king.'
Pilate asked him, 'Are you the king of the Jews?'
'So you say,' answered Jesus. Then Pilate said
to the chief priests and the crowds, 'I find no
reason to condemn this man.' But they insisted
even more strongly. So Pilate passed the sentence
on Jesus that they were asking for.

Master of the Bruges Passion Scenes,
Christ presented to the People

The Way to Calvary

O all ye who pass by, behold and see;
Man stole the fruit, but I must climb the tree;
The tree of life to all, but only me.
'The Sacrifice', George Herbert

The soldiers took Jesus inside to the courtyard
of the governor's palace and called together the
rest of the company. They put a purple robe on
Jesus, made a crown out of thorny branches, and
put it on his head. Then they began to salute him:
'Long live the king of the Jews!' They beat him
over the head with a stick, spat on him, fell on
their knees, and bowed down to him. When they
had finished mocking him, they took off the purple
robe and put his own clothes back on him. Then
they led him out to crucify him.

Ambrogio Bergognone,
Christ carrying the Cross

The Crucifixion

But, O my God, my God! why leav'st thou me,
The son, in whom thou dost delight to be?
My God, my God –
Never was grief like mine.

'The Sacrifice', George Herbert

They took Jesus to a place called Golgotha,
which means 'The Place of the Skull'. Then they
crucified him and divided his clothes among
themselves, throwing dice to see who would get
which piece of clothing. It was nine o'clock in
the morning when they crucified him. The notice
of the accusation against him said, 'The King of
the Jews'. At noon the whole country was covered
with darkness, which lasted for three hours. At
three o'clock Jesus cried out with a loud shout,
'Eloi, Eloi, lema sabachthani?' which means, 'My
God, my God, why did you abandon me?' With
a loud cry Jesus died.

Antonello da Messina,
Christ Crucified

The Deposition

O blessed body! Whither art thou thrown?
No lodging for thee, but a cold hard stone?
So many hearts on earth, and yet not one
Receive thee?

'Sepulchre', George Herbert

There was a man named Joseph from Arimathea,
a town in Judea. He was a good and honourable
man, who was waiting for the coming of the
Kingdom of God. Although he was a member of
the Council, he had not agreed with their decision
and action. He went into the presence of Pilate
and asked for the body of Jesus. Then he took
the body down, wrapped it in a linen sheet, and
placed it in a tomb which had been dug out of
solid rock and which had never been used. It was
Friday, and the Sabbath was about to begin.

Ugolino di Nerio,
The Deposition

The Resurrection

Rise heart; thy Lord is risen. Sing his praise
Without delays.

'Easter', George Herbert

Very early on Sunday morning the women went
to the tomb, carrying the spices they had prepared.
They found the stone rolled away from the
entrance to the tomb, so they went in; but they
did not find the body of the Lord Jesus. They
stood there puzzled about this, when suddenly
two men in bright shining clothes stood by them.
Full of fear, the women bowed down to the ground,
as the men said to them, 'Why are you looking
among the dead for one who is alive? He is not
here; he has been raised. Remember what he said
to you while he was in Galilee: "The Son of Man
must be handed over to sinners, be crucified, and
three days later rise to life." '

Attributed to Jacopo di Cione,
The Maries at the Sepulchre

The Ascension

His state
Is kingly: thousands at his bidding speed,
And post o'er land and ocean without rest;
They also serve who only stand and wait.
'On his blindness', John Milton

Suddenly the Lord himself stood among the disciples and said to them, 'Peace be with you.' Then he opened their minds to understand the Scriptures, and said to them, 'This is what is written: the Messiah must suffer and must rise from death three days later, and in his name the message about repentance and the forgiveness of sins must be preached to all nations, beginning in Jerusalem. You are witnesses of these things.' After saying this, he was taken up to heaven as they watched him, and a cloud hid him from their sight.

To him be glory, power, praise,
From this, unto the last of days.
'Easter Hymn', Henry Vaughan

Fra Angelico,
Christ Glorified in the Court of Heaven

Text acknowledgments

5: John 14:19. 8: Luke 1:26–27, 30–32. 10: Luke 2:1, 3–7. 12: Luke 2:25–30.
14: Luke 2:41–47. 16: Matthew 3:1–2, 13–16. 18: John 2:1–3, 7–10. 20: Luke
9:28–31, 34–35. 22: Luke 10:38–42. 24: John 8:2–5, 7, 9. 26: John 11:1, 3, 17,
32, 38–39, 43–44. 28: Matthew 21:10–13. 30: Mark 14:17–18, 22–26. 32: Mark
14:32, 35–36, 40, 41–43. 34: Mark 14:53, 60–64. 36: Luke 23:1–5, 24. 38: Mark
15:16–20. 40: Mark 15:22, 24–26, 33–34, 37. 42: Luke 23:50–54. 44: Luke 24:1–7.
46: Luke 24:36, 45–48; Acts 1:9.

Scripture quotations are taken from the Good News Bible published by The Bible
Societies/HarperCollins Publishers Ltd, UK © American Bible Society 1966, 1971,
1976, 1992, used with permission. Spelling and punctuation of quotations may have
been modernized.

Picture acknowledgments

All pictures in this book are details. Copyright © The National Gallery, London.

Cover, 6: NG 673 Christ Blessing, Antonello da Messina. 8–9: NG 3068.1 The
Annunciation: The Angel Gabriel, Gaudenzio Ferrari. 10–11: NG 1034 'Mystic
Nativity', Sandro Botticelli. 12–13: L 34 The Presentation of Jesus in the Temple,
Guercino. 14–15: NG 1495 Christ disputing with the Doctors, Lodovico Mazzolino.
16–17: NG 665 The Baptism of Christ, Piero della Francesca. 18–19: NG 6372
The Marriage at Cana, Mattia Preti. 20–21: NG 1330 The Transfiguration, Duccio.
22–23: NG 1375 Kitchen Scene with Christ in the House of Martha and Mary,
Diego Velázquez. 24–25: NG 45 The Woman taken in Adultery, Rembrandt.
26–27: NG 1 The Raising of Lazarus, Sebastiano del Piombo. 28–29: NG 1194
The Purification of the Temple, after Michelangelo. 30–31: NG 1127 The Institution
of the Eucharist, Ercole de' Roberti. 32–33: NG 1417 The Agony in the Garden,
Andrea Mantegna. 34–35: NG 3679 Christ before the High Priest, Gerrit van
Honthorst. 36–37: NG 1087 Christ presented to the People, Master of the Bruges
Passion Scenes. 38–39: NG 1077.2 Christ carrying the Cross, Ambrogio Bergognone.
40–41: NG 1166 Christ Crucified, Antonello da Messina. 42–43: NG 3375 The
Deposition, Ugolino di Nerio. 44–45: NG 576 The Maries at the Sepulchre,
attributed to Jacopo di Cione and workshop. 46–47: NG 663.1 Christ Glorified
in the Court of Heaven, Fra Angelico.

MYSTERY OF CATS

written and illustrated by

DAVID WESTWOOD

TWO HEADS PUBLISHING

WELCOME
TO THE
WONDERFUL
WORLD OF
CATS...

SMUDGE

Thanks to
John Berley, Robert Bloomfield, Janet Bonthron,
Sharon Dirnberger, Marilyn Fleming, Charles Frewin, Rudy Garza,
Susan Kelly, Kathy Toguchi and the resources of the vast
Toguchi Cat Library, Mike Rossi, and of course little Schmickels.

The History of Felines

The great open spaces
where cats are cats.

— *Don Marquis, mehitabel has an adventure*

To hear humans talk, you'd think we only came on the scene in 3000BC, when the Egyptians are supposed to have 'tamed' us. Or, according to some more recent discoveries, in Cyprus 3000 years earlier. What really happened in history is, of course, a little different. From a more felinocentric point of view, this is the way it went:

Millions of years ago, the cat's giant ancestor *Felixosaurus rex* ruled the earth, scourge of all beasts, master of mammal and reptile alike. Its massive whiskers swept the savannah, its yawn trapped entire flocks of pterodactyls, its roar dwarfed the volcanoes. Dogosaurs cringed cravenly in its wake.

But after a while all the dinosaurs died out, the most current theory being that their flatulence caused global warming, disrupting the food chain.

Whatever the rea-
son, Nature
favoured a smaller
scale, and the next
incarnation of
catkind, the sabre-
tooths, held sway
for a few more
æons. They began
the era of what are
now known as the
'big' cats, who
roamed at will,
unchallenged
emperors of the
earth.

Until, that is, hominids came on the scene.
Out of the forests and jungles wobbled these
bandy-legged bipeds who, tired of a vegetarian
diet, foolishly tried to compete with *us*, the kings
and queens of the hunt.

We weren't too concerned at first. They didn't
seem much of a threat. Slow, noisy and smelling of
old sweat, we could sense them coming half a con-

tinent away. Besides, there was plenty of game to go round, and who wants woolly mammoth hide in the teeth anyway? No, if they stayed to themselves we weren't going to bother with them, ugly things.

But when they started to trap us, that was different. Something had to be done, and the sabretooths got together and slapped around a few of the Big Stupids, or, as we call them now, Neanderthals. Not being the brightest creatures they didn't get the message. Then the big cats tried herding these proto-humans in the hope that they could be taught to serve and make some use of themselves, but with no luck. Neanderthals turned out to be good at bashing things over the head, especially each other, but very little else. There was nothing to do but eat them, and they didn't even taste very good — tough, stringy, and funkier than even *we* like our meat.

So that took care of the Neanderthal. (And paleontologists wonder what the scratches on their bones are. 'Burial rituals' indeed.) But another group of hominids, now called the Cro-Magnons but then known to our forebears as Bigs, in turn ambushed the sabretooths in an effort to ensure their own safety. And, shameful though it is for us to admit, they succeeded. There were probably a few fillets of feline on Cro-Magnon cave fires for a while. This was also the start of several thousand years of making coats out of us.

The remaining big cats — the lion, panther, cheetah, leopard, carnivores so magnificently adapted to their environment that they still exist today — thenceforth resolved to avoid humans whenever they could, making only occasional forays into twoleg territory only when other, better quarry was unavailable.

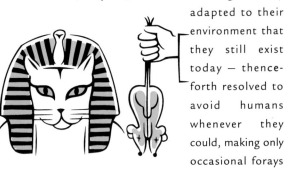

And that would have been the end of any ongoing interaction between the two species if not for the development of another branch of the cat family — the smaller cats. Equally carnivorous, and equally supreme as hunters, but of smaller prey.

These European and African wildcats dined on rodents, and when humans finally discovered agriculture (we tried to show the Bigs but it didn't take), rodents in turn discovered what they grew. First of all in the fields, and then, when societies like that of the Egyptians started to have surplus enough to store, in the granaries.

The wildcats followed their food, and found it in abundance where the new human farmers kept theirs. Rodentville. Verminland. Mouse City. Rat-O-Rama.

Why slog around the grasslands, the wildcats thought, getting burrs in our fur, stepping on thorns? Why chase mice that run down holes when we could just hang out by the bins and pick 'em off at our leisure? And pick them off we did. When you consider that rodents can eat a third to a half of a harvest, you can begin to imagine how many pickings there are. And when you consider that a cat can ingest 7000 mice or 4000 rats per year...

This went down well with the Egyptians. They became our first friends. When they weren't building pyramids and mummifying pharaohs to stick in them, they worshipped — us. OK, so they also deified dung beetles, but they understandably appreciated our mysteriousness, our aloofness, our grace, more than any other animal. They were the first New Agers, after all, into other worlds and what comes after death and psychic powers and spells and all that stuff. We were, to them, the very embodiment of magic.

And for a couple of millennia we were top of the heap. Cats were protected by law, and anyone caught killing a cat was condemned to death. (Someone coming across a dead cat would run away in fear of being thought the cause of its demise.) We were memorialised in art, mummified like the kings and queens — even the poor paid for a funeral for their cats, shaving off their eyebrows in their grief. Adolescents tattooed the cat-goddess Bastet on their arms to attract her gifts.

Eventually, of course, we were smuggled out by the Phœnicians to Greece, brought west by the Romans and introduced to the rest of a delighted world.

We became everyone's household hunter, the original stealth fighter, the Rolls Royce of pest control. The Pest Ingester. The Verminator. And not just hunters, either. We were valued as guardians who bestowed good fortune and protection on households and crops alike. It was the Golden Age of Cats.

But it couldn't last. After the 10th century the cold and humourless grip of The Church descended on Europe and its colonies, pegging cats as instruments or incarnations of the Devil, and along with so-called 'witches' the cat was chosen as

scapegoat for an entire paranoid population. Popes even officially sanctioned this reign of terror. For hundreds of years friendly, harmless, useful domestic cats were hunted, maimed, burned, buried alive, walled into buildings, hanged and thrown from towers. It was not exactly suburbia. It was Catastrophe.

This vicious period only succeeded, inevitably, in allowing rodents to run rampant. Without their predators mice were free to munch crops to their stomach's content, and rats multiplied at alarming rates along with their passengers, the fleas. The fleas carried the plagues, and promptly bit all the humans they could find, wiping out, at conservative estimates, a third of Europe's population.

Only in the East were cats still revered, and that's why so many more breeds — Persian, Angora, Siamese, etc — came out of the Orient.

So the cat purges of the Middle Ages backfired on *Homo sapiens*, serving to prove that that we were beneficial, our mutual alliance a positive one. Even so, it wasn't until the late 18th and early 19th centuries that the cat became a darling of the French beau monde. And not until the Victorian era were we fully reinstated to our monarchy of the hearth. We were saved by sentimentality. We  regained the respect of the bipeds, if at the cost of some of our dignity. We were thought of as ornaments, pretty pets, toys — symbols of a successful bourgeoisie, along with pianos, antimacassars and potted palms. But at least we weren't flayed alive. Better fed than dead.

And throughout the twentieth century we became more and more popular, bringing our lovable qualities and predatory predilections into grateful homes everywhere. From Kitty Hawk to Kitakyushu, Catalonia to Catalina, Katanga to Katmandu cats can now be seen gracing the windows, porches, verandahs, decks and drives of all kinds of dwelling, from poor to prosperous, slum to stately home. We are gatto, gato, gata; we are katt, katze, koshka; we are catta, cait, chat. We have become ubiquitous.

Now, of course, humans worship us again, as well they should. They write musicals, poems (hopefully not doggerel) and endless numbers of books about us, parade us in special shows and award us prizes, and — the ultimate accolade — name cars after us.

But it's hardly surprising. After all, the descendants of the Big Stupids — no longer stupid, but still big — have little class and less style. They have to learn it from somewhere, and that's why God created Cat.

Cat Years

Nothing's more playful than a young cat,
nor more grave than an old one.
— *Thomas Fuller*

This chart shows the approximate correlations between cat years and human. (Sorry — the traditional multiplication of the cat's age by 7 doesn't work.)

FELIS CATUS		HOMO SAPIENS
1	infancy-adolescence	**15**
2	youth	**25**
4	early middle age	**40**
7	late middle age	**50**
10	senior	**60**
15	getting on a bit	**75**
20	definitely pushing it	**105**
30	forget it	**120**

Average lifespan 10 years.
Average time awake 3 years.
Longest substantiated lifespan 36.

Evolution of the Domestic Cat

Felixosaurus rex

Dean of the Dinosauria. One angry sweep of its twenty-meter tail could level a small forest. Coughed up hairballs the size of buses. To fuel its enormous bulk, it's estimated that *Felixosaurus* was required to catch 130,000 rodents or 90,000 medium-sized fish per day to survive. It consequently died out long before the other dinosaurs from either lack of food or exhaustion.

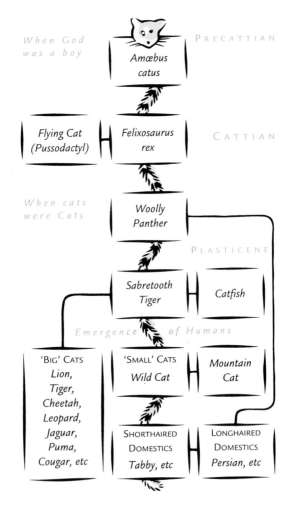

When God
was a boy

*Amœbus
catus*

PRECATTIAN

Flying Cat
(Pussodactyl)

*Felixosaurus
rex*

CATTIAN

When cats
were Cats

*Woolly
Panther*

PLASTICENE

*Sabretooth
Tiger*

Catfish

Emergence   of Humans

'BIG' CATS
*Lion,
Tiger,
Cheetah,
Leopard,
Jaguar,
Puma,
Cougar, etc*

'SMALL' CATS
Wild Cat

*Mountain
Cat*

SHORTHAIRED
DOMESTICS
Tabby, etc

LONGHAIRED
DOMESTICS
Persian, etc

Woolly Panther *(Panthera hirsutus)*

This massive and powerful beast was the ancestor of the Persian. Its magnificent coat is thought to have measured an average of 6 metres in length, but turned out to be its downfall. Once wet, the additional weight of soggy fur unfortunately immobilised the animal. This meant that during a prolonged rainstorm or accidental immersion in a swamp or river, it couldn't move, catch food and eat. If starvation didn't get them, mildew did.

Sabretooth Tiger *(Eusmilus dentata)*

The feline with the canines. Had a tendency to trip over its own teeth. Is thought to have become extinct partly from trapping by Stone Age man, and from the males accidentally castrating themselves whilst cleaning their nether regions.

Catfish *(Felis aquatica)*

   This adaptation of cats to water, possibly trig-
gered by a desperate attempt to get as close as
possible to fish, led to the loss of almost all feline
characteristics except for whiskers. These sad speci-
mens are now relegated to scuttling around the
bottom of rivers and lakes, humiliating examples of
greed-induced devolution.

Tibetan Mountain Cat *(Felis everestus)*

The Times reported in 1950 that a 4-month old cat accompanied a group of climbers scaling the 14,780ft Matterhorn. This almost certainly was the last verifiable report of a 'Sherpa' Cat, once common in the Himalayas before the Chinese invasion of Tibet. Popular for centuries with mountain climbers of all nations, these tireless alpine-adapted creatures were prized for their persistence, sure-footedness and warmth in a sleeping bag.

The first and only experiment with Cat Sleds

Cat Diet

Do cats eat bats?.. Do bats eat cats?
— Lewis Carroll

Evil-smelling things in overpriced little tins

Mice and rats

Squirrels, small rabbits, moles

Birds (especially pets)

Fish (especially pets)

Spiders, beetles, flies

Butterflies and moths

Frogs

Bubbles

Wool

Garbage

Paper

Expensive shoes

Expensive belts

Shoelaces

Flowers

Houseplants and the herbs in the windowbox

...and anything that moves in an
interesting way.

Identifying your Cat's Mood

Gaze with those bright languid segments green, and prick those
velvet ears — but prythee do not stick thy latent talons in me...
— *John Keats, To Mrs Reynolds' Cat*

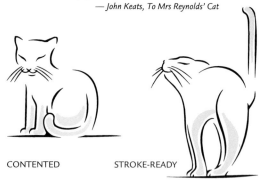

CONTENTED   STROKE-READY

WASHTIME   ANGRY

CATNAP

READY TO POUNCE

FRISKY

CARELESS

Tailography

Self-expression with your caudal appendage

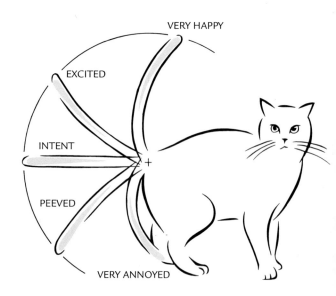

VERY HAPPY

EXCITED

INTENT

PEEVED

VERY ANNOYED

THE BASIC POSITIONS

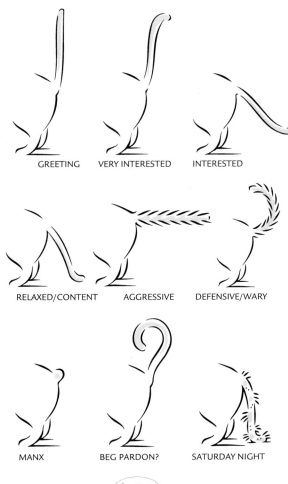

GREETING   VERY INTERESTED   INTERESTED

RELAXED/CONTENT   AGGRESSIVE   DEFENSIVE/WARY

MANX   BEG PARDON?   SATURDAY NIGHT

Earography

Wasn't that the can opener?

HAPPY,
OR AT LEAST NOT *UN*HAPPY

ANGRY

FRIGHTENED,
OR SCOTTISH FOLD

LISTENING TO
SOMETHING BEHIND

Whiskerography

Vibes from the ol' vibrissae

MILITARY

ENGLISH

LOUIS XIV

PUNK, REX or TOO NEAR THE STOVE

MALE MATING DISPLAY

The Nine Lives of a Cat

Ding dong, bell
Pussy's in the well
— *Traditional English children's rhyme*

THE PLAYFUL LIFE

Lost to playing with objects, like lawnmowers, that didn't play back.

THE CURIOUS LIFE

Lost to inquisitiveness about situations, like the open oven door, that should never have been looked into.

THE TERRITORIAL LIFE

Lost in battle with other, bigger, meaner, cats.

THE EXPLORING LIFE

Lost to motor vehicles whilst seeing if the grass really is greener.

THE MACHO LIFE

Lost in battle with a psychotic dog that wasn't afraid of claws.

THE SPORTING LIFE

Lost by falling into river while reaching for those fascinating little fish.

THE SKYDIVING LIFE

Lost in misjudging the distance between the fifteenth floor flat and street level.

THE MEDICAL LIFE

Lost in battle with those annoying stowaways, the internal parasites.

THE SENIOR CITIZEN LIFE

Lost to old age, passing on to that Big Lap in the Sky.

Reigning Cats and Dogs

*The cat, an aristocrat, merits our esteem, while the dog only...
got his position by low flatteries.*
— *Alexandre Dumas*

Dogs became pets around 45,000 years ago by hanging around campfires and giving up their individuality in return for a few scraps of gristle and the odd bone or two. On the other hand, though cats appeared on earth over ten *million* years ago, we *never* gave up our identity.

Experts in animal behaviour might try to tell you that the difference lies in the genes: dogs evolved as pack animals who bring down their prey in cooperative groups, and so were programmed to get along with others. Cats, on the other hand, are by nature solitary hunters, and so are genetically unequipped for social behaviour.

This, as any cat knows, is errant nonsense. Cats can behave socially when we want to — we're just shrewder. Recognising our dog cousins' enslavement for what it was, we adopted our 'I'm doing you a favour by just allowing you to house and feed me' attitude. (In fact, it is now acknowledged that we *invented* attitude, along with yoga and mood swings.) Why else would it have taken us *forty thousand years* longer than dogs to hang out with humankind? No, the feline species chose humans to use as hosts, not masters, and at best are only ever houseguests and never slaves. We're

just as social as any other species, but where dogs idolise, we patronise. Dogs fawn; we scorn. Besides, dogs made the classic army mistake — they *volunteered*.

Eventually cats decided on our present eminently successful method — *pretending* to be pets, while using hominids as unwitting serfs.

In this manner cats now only have to hunt for fun, as anyone who's ever seen a cat playing with a mouse will attest. No longer do we need to work for a living, since our food comes out of cans, and our longest trek is now from the top shelf of the entertainment centre to the patch of sun on the kitchen windowsill.

Dogs, on the other hand, have to sit, stay, fetch, carry, lie down, beg, shake hands, roll over, play dead, herd, guard, point, sniff, retrieve and all those other mundane duties of their kind. They've become an *appendage* to man, subject to his whims and orders. And they get their ears in their food.

But have we cats still sold out our independence in choosing human hosts? This is the subject of ongoing debates in feline circles, sometimes leading to those heated discussions in the middle of the night outside your bedroom window. Are dogs better off? Have canines done better out of their association? We have only one word in response:

Poodles.

*The first and only
experiment with
Poodlecuts
for Persians*

Canines vs Felines

DOGS	**CATS**
Howl.	Yowl.
Can be trained to do tricks.	Talk to my agent.
Friendly, cooperative.	Selfish, indifferent.
Can detect and deter intruders.	Will allow intruders to stroke, then yawn and nap.
Will mark everything, forever.	Will spray everything, until fixed.
Will eat until they puke, if allowed.	Will only eat what we need. Usually.

DOGS	**CATS**
Can herd animals.	Will attack animals.
Like to be taken for walks.	Walk? Why? It's raining.
Want to please.	Want to be waited on.
Will fetch.	Moi? Surely you jest.
Yap, bark, yelp, growl, slaver, pant.	Please. How crass.
Beg.	Tickle my tummy, would you? Ahhh, that's it. Just there.

The first and only
experiment with
Guide Cats for the Blind

Cat Camouflage

> Can the Ethiopian change his skin,
> or the Leopard change his spots?
> — *Bible, Jeremiah*

Far from being the random result of mixed genetic inheritance, feline markings are actually cunning adaptations to the modern world. Evolving faster than almost any other organism, each cat comes in a variety superbly and opportunistically suited to its environment.

TABBY/MACKEREL/AGOUTI (brown and black in irregular stripes or blotches.) To be able to hide amongst trees and bushes and pounce on unsuspecting birds.

SPOTTED TABBY (Ocelot or Leopardlike)
Bad wallpaper, polkadot clothing

SHORTHAIRED WHITE To blend with snow, fog, flour.

CHINCHILLA/WHITE PERSIAN (fluffy white) To sleep undisturbed amongst fur coats, pillows, angora sweaters, yetis, and on sheepskin seatcovers.

BLACK, or **BLUE** (grey-blue) To be able to remain indistinguishable in cellars, rubbish bins, shadows and during nocturnal sexual liaisons.

SOLID POINT (Siamese/seal/chocolate/blue — pale grey or cream with black or brown face and paws)
To merge with bamboo.

TORTOISESHELL (red and black irregular patches) and **CALICO** (fawn and black) To be able to disguise ourselves in sock drawers, on half-dead lawns, badly-patched driveways, hospital operating room floors and accidents in the kitchen.

Cat Social Classes

A cat's social standing can't solely be assessed by colour or length of coat. And since cats mate less discriminately than humans, the only reliable identifying mark of social standing is thus our name, which shows what kind of nest we're from.

boudoir/show

The Pedigreed Ones: Polysyllabic names like Satinpennypuss Amberglowmistmuff, Apricotcreaméclair Honeybuncurd, Fudgebucket Catnip Squitsmeister, Pastelpockets Downyheather, Jamdoughnut Heathburton, Scheherazade von Sandringham, Blancmangelette Bertinaboots, etc.

bohemian

Artsy or political names like Tolstoi, Isolde, Buxtehude, Warhol, Goethe, Thelonious, Che, Kierkegaard, Madame Bovary, Rasputin, Mao, Fibonacci, Schwartzenegger, etc.

house/family

Standard, honest cat names like Sooty, Smoky, Brandy, Fluffy, Whisky, Tiger, Marmaduke, Marmalade, Socks, Bootsie, Patches, Lady Di, etc.

farm

Dry, boring names like The Cat, Kitty, Fred, Jane, Turd, etc.

stray/alley

The most basic of labels: Hey you! Getouttahere! Shutthehellup! Whatthehellsthatracket! Etc.

MARMALADE   02.05.94   2a

Cat Mythology

Only imbeciles do not know that
all cats have a pact with the Devil.
— *L'Evangile du Diable*

Cats are instruments of the Devil

Europeans in the Middle Ages associated cats with paganism, as witches' familiars or magical servants, witches in another form, marking a path to the Devil or even an embodiment of Satan himself. Witches were even killed with their cats.

As if this weren't enough, cats were thought to cause storms and wreck ships, desecrate crucifixes and turn beer sour. Many thought ridding the world of cats would rid them of ills, and cat stew became popular. But all they managed to rid themselves of was their most effective rat predator, and exacerbated the plagues by the subsequent proliferation of rodent-carried fleas.

In 1344, the entire population of Metz, Germany, was overtaken by an epidemic of St Vitus' Dance. A pious knight-at-arms, presumably wanting to have a good laugh at all these people flailing around, visited and took a room at an inn. There he found a black cat sitting in the fireplace, staring at him. The knight promptly made the sign of the cross and lunged for his sword. The cat is supposed to have spat blasphemies and disappeared into thin air. (As if any sane animal would stay and be decapitated.) Predictably, Mr Knight thought he'd seen the Devil, and when the town

was miraculously cured the next day he told the town magistrates and they organised a ritual cat burning.

Every eve of St John thereafter, thirteen living cats were thrown on a huge bonfire. These barbaric barbecues, the Fires of St John, lasted 429 years, when in 1773 a Mme d'Armentières obtained us a reprieve. To this day, many a cat still gives up a little prayer to the great Madame, as it appreciates the distance between itself and the living room fire.

Black cats are lucky

Because of the silly satanic associations, most countries believe a black cat crossing one's path is unlucky. The British, cleverly ignoring this calumny, think it leads to *good* luck. This superstition appears to date from the writings of one Samuel Twerfle, an English manure-spreader's apprentice whom church records show died in Buggersby, Shropshire in 1408. Twerfle was apparently obsessed with a neighbour's black cat, who tended to appear periodically at his window. Whenever it did, Mrs Twerfle suddenly seemed unusually interested in 'performinge her nuptyal expectationnes,' which endeared the cat to Samuel.

Later, Sam changed his mind when the same cat tangled itself in his ankles, causing him to become deeply immersed in his work. But by then the damage was done, his rumours had spread abroad, and the black cat's good luck was legend, at least in Britain. Other countries are still hampered by the old Mediæval superstitions of evil.

Cats invented Yoga

An old Indian story describes how a young

prince named Hatha was having trouble concentrating on his difficult Karma Yoga meditation exercises. (Karma Yoga involves getting in touch with one's previous incarnations and teaching *them* how to meditate too.) To clear his mind he went for a walk in the woods and came across a cat, sitting straight on a tree stump.

When he asked the cat how she could meditate so peacefully, she showed him how she stretched each muscle, twisting and arching, tensing and relaxing until her whole body was at rest and released from distractions.

Every day the prince returned and learned the cat's technique, eventually spreading his knowledge to others as Hatha's Yoga. In fact, he opened a chain of Hatha Yoga centres throughout Asia, becoming rich, famous and fat. Meanwhile the poor cat, though superbly relaxed, died from malnutrition in the forest.

A cat has nine lives

This misconception probably stems from our ability to land on our feet, often narrowly escaping becoming purr purée. (But only if we have time to turn around in mid-air so our feet are down. Paradoxically, a longer fall, within reason, is safer than a very short one.) This gave rise to the belief that cats have the power to cheat death.

But stay away from those who wish to test this.

Cats have a sixth sense

Only six? Cats have *dozens* of senses, not to mention more *common* sense than most animals. Our sense of smell tells us what we're near without seeing it, exactly how far away it is, whether it's edible, and even when it last had a bath. Our vision enables us to see in bright sunlight, dim light, next to no light, and even red-light districts. Our sense of balance is so refined that we rarely put a foot wrong (and we can't even *see* two of them), even in the most delicate of situations. Well, hot tin roofs aside.

Cats can see in the dark

Cat's eyes are designed to operate with far less light than humans, which makes us seem to the superstitious to be able to see in total darkness, our eyes appearing to glow from the reflection of what little light there might be. (Primates, being diurnal creatures, are incapacitated by the dark and remain afraid of the night.) Nor are cats usually hampered by the unfortunate mechanism that makes rabbits and deer freeze like statues in the face of dangers like car headlights, turning them into road pizza.

This plus the fact that we have no collarbones in order to facilitate the navigation of narrow, dark areas, and that our whiskers are the width of the body so we can find our way around even when blind made cats appear endowed with supernatural powers.

We *are* supernatural, of course. Supernaturally beautiful.

Curiosity killed the cat

We cats are relentlessly, incorrigibly, wonderfully curious. Originally a positive survival trait

used for tracking prey and
exploring, our peculiarly
intense feline inquisitiveness can now have, in
some situations, the oppo-
site value. Every day med-
dling moggies meet untimely ends by being in the
wrong place at the wrong time: under cars, under
car bonnets, in rubbish bins prior to pickup, fool-
ing with the prop of the grand piano lid, etc. In our
focus on the fascination of the moment we can
sometimes lose sight of the larger picture. Like the
train coming.

Cats can find their way home over great distances

Countless examples of this ability are record-
ed, and not all can be dismissed as the mere fol-
lowing of a scent trail.

An army sergeant was transferred from
Kokomo, Indiana to Augusta, Georgia, and took
his cat by train with him. The cat made it back to
its original home, a distance of 700 miles, in three
weeks. If you've ever been to Augusta, you'll under-

·stand what motivated this clever creature.

Moumousse was lost during his 'owner's' holiday in Maine-et-Loire, France. Ten months later he returned to his master's house in Doubs, 465 miles away. And why not? Moumousse had fifteen lovers there.

And **Sugar**, a cream semi-Persian living in Anderson, California, was left behind with a neighbour when her family moved to Oklahoma. Fourteen months later, Sugar had somehow crossed half a continent — 1500 miles — to be reunited with them.

Then there was **Chat Beau**, who travelled 300 miles from Lafayette, Louisiana to Texarkana, Texas in 4 months. **Pooh**, 2 years old, 200 miles between Newman, Georgia and Wellford, South Carolina. **Smoky**, 417 miles from Tulsa, Oklahoma to Memphis, Tennessee in 12 months. **Rusty**, who managed the 950 miles from Boston, Massachusetts to Chicago, Illinois. **Howie**, 1000 miles across the Australian Outback to Adelaide. And **McCavity**, who trekked 500 miles from Scotland to Cornwall.

Currently being investigated is the iron in the cat's body working as a kind of compass. Not under investigation, unfortunately, is the iron *will* of felines to be in comfort. How long does it take for humans to grasp that if we don't like it, we're outta there?

Cats can read minds

This superstition possibly stems from the observation that cats are the only domestic animal that can look a human in the eye without flinching. But far from being a result of telepathy, it is a result of supreme *apathy*. Nothing could conceivably interest us *less* than the contents of a ape's mind, which we consider somewhat intellectually inferior.

Ancient Britons believed that if you gazed into a cat's eyes you could see into the spirit world — an inheritance, perhaps, from the Egyptians, who were fascinated with cat's eyes and whose word for the animal, *mau*, meant 'to see.' Personally, though, we'd rather not be stared at, spirit world or no. It's upsetting to be confronted at such close quarters by such vacancy.

It's bad luck to cross a stream with a cat in your arms

This inane French proverb isn't too hard to understand. You might as well say it's bad luck to light a match in a firework factory. Anyone with a modicum of smarts knows that nearly all cats hate water. (There are exceptions, but we don't talk about that side of the family.) Therefore, if you're foolish enough to try to carry a cat across a large body of the stuff you'd better be prepared for some serious lacerations. The cat would obviously be concerned that the human, whom we consider more than a little uncoordinated, would drop it. And we prefer our water measured in bowlsful, thanks.

The Manx originally had a tail

According to legend, the Manx was late to the launch of Noah's Ark, and Noah accidentally slammed the door on its gloriously bushy tail.

Assuming for the moment that the story of Noah's Ark is true, it's extremely unlikely that any self-respecting cat would be late to get aboard. For a start, since we hate water it's not hard to guess that one of us would do anything to avoid being caught in a worldwide *flood* of the revolting stuff. Secondly, while Cap'n No is said to have included only pairs of animals, any cat would be smart enough to calculate that it wouldn't be long before there were plenty more than just two each of the rats and mice aboard, and wouldn't have missed the chance of such captive chow.

Cats can predict earthquakes

Cats often do anticipate earthquakes because our refined senses and sensitive whiskers can detect vibrations long before the Bigs get an inkling that something's wrong. By the time they're being bombarded by flying saucepans we're usually safely out

of the window or under the bed. (**Toto**, living in the foothills of Vesuvius, gave his hosts so much warning of the volcano's impending eruption that all escaped safely.)

Prior to recent...er...*cata*clysms in California, groups of shrewd cats apparently got together and jumped freight trains out of state, hitchhiked on excursion buses to Las Vegas, and stowed away on a cruise ship to Acapulco.

The lynx can see through walls

During the Middle Ages, several strange legends spread through Europe about the lynx. Apart from its supposed x-ray vision it was also thought to be huge and its urine to crystallise into gemstones, which shows how few people can have actually seen one. We can presume some mediæval lynx pee-pursuers to have been severely disappointed. You might want to check that amber necklace, though.

Cats are manipulative pets

This libel really has to stop. We just know what we want, that's all. Anyone who wants a pet without a mind should stick with jerboas or goldfish.

Besides, we provide something humans seem to have trouble giving each other: *love*. To good humans, we felines are as faithful as any hound, and add to the home our personalities, our perfection, and...well...our purrs.

also available in the same series:

HUMANS AS PETS

KITTICULTURE

by David Westwood,
author of THE OFFICE MANUAL *and* THE LOVE MANUAL

TWO HEADS PUBLISHING
12A Franklyn Suite, The Priory
Haywards Heath, West Sussex RH16 3LB

Text and illustrations © 1994 David Westwood, all rights reserved

ISBN 1 897850 95 6

Printed in Great Britain by Caldra House Ltd., Hove, Sussex
Bound by Butler & Tanner, Somerset